An Empowerment Journal for Women through a Spiritual Birth

"IT WAS THEN THAT I REALIZED I WAS CREATING ℒIFE AS ETERNAL ℒOVE."

Date of Birth: _____

Time: _____

©2020 by Roni Hopkins
All rights reserved.
ISBN: 978-1-7349035-5-3

About the Author

Roni Hopkins is the creator of a unique collection of journals that specialize in spirituality and consciousness. She has traveled the world, connecting with all walks of life and lives her purpose dedicated to assisting others on their journey. The creation of these journals reflect those experiences and bring a level of universal insight to ones own spiritual path. These journals encourage you to discover and express your truth, wisdom and ever evolving awareness throughout the pages and beyond them through our virtual discussions.

Every path reveals its truth within you.

www.RoniHopkins.com

As a woman, pregnancy is the most natural and created form of our physical being. From conception through development and giving birth, it is a process of life that our bodies instinctively and intuitively know how to do. It is the one experience that leaves all control in the realm of the Divine.

And from the moment this process begins, we become the canvas of infinite creation at work. It is miraculous, it is transcendence and it holds no comparison to any other experience of life here on earth. It shifts us into realms that we are opened to receiving not only life, but all that is eternal as a *Gift* of creation in this physical world.

You were chosen.

As much as pregnancy is a physical transformation of our lives, we also have to gain clarity of the spiritual component to truly understand the fullness of what this process is for a woman. Too often, women go through pregnancy only with the perspective of physical reproduction and when a physical life is not produced, we suffer and are left with a drastic spiritual undertaking without any understanding of the greater purpose of life that it gave us.

The key is to discover the gift that was created for you from the experience and honoring the creation of life in every form.

You are the divine connection between all of life that exist in the earth. You hold no limitations to the life that can come through you, as all life created is an eternal expression of the Divine.

It illuminates your soul from conception and flows throughout your being. It creates a oneness that reaches into all that is living and existing in the earth. You are a creator of life and no matter how it manifest, it is yours to cherish and honor in every way. It is truly a gift of *Creation* and *Love*.

This is your Gift to Express

Your Experiences

Your Reflections

Your Love.

"Make yourself a Priority and not a Sacrifice."

As women, we often place ourselves secondary to the day to day priorities of life. During this time, it is mistaken for others to see that our lives are anything other than normal, since much of this experience transforms us from within. It can leave our physical life seamless without any change at all.

The importance of taking care of your well being is essential to the synergistic balance and healing of the natural flow of life.

As we breathe in, We take in Life.
As we breathe out , We give Life.

The imbalance of either giving or taking causes a displacement in spirit, mind and body. You cannot give from an empty vessel. Sacrifice displays strength but also a position of depletion. It is not sustainable to operate daily from this state when you deserve you more than anything.

Date:

I am LOVE.

Date:

I am BALANCE.

Date:

"Allow the renewal of your soul, mind and body be the focal point of what you see."

I am COMPASSION.

Date:

I am DIVINE.

Date:

I am BRAVE.

Date:

"There is a perfect purpose in ALL of life created."

There is purpose for everything we experience in life. No matter how it makes us feel, those feelings do not dictate the true purpose of the reasons.

Life is never creating against you in any way. It is always creating for us to experience the fullness of all the possibilities of the life we have been given.

Even in the process of creating life, we are expanding ourselves beyond the physical to create from this perfection.

Date:

I am HEALTHY.

Date:

I am PEACE.

Date:

"Everything happens exactly as it should, though we may not understand the reasons, it is for those reasons all of your Life has meaning."

I am AUTHENTIC.

Date:

I am GRACE.

Date:

I am SERENITY.

Date:

"All souls come from an existence that is beyond our will to control it."

Every soul that desires to have a life here on earth comes here in perfect timing. Though we often perceive it as our child and our creation, we have to remember that it operates autonomously as its own existence and it comes only to have this human experience in whatever capacity it is destined to be.

As we also have come here to experience our own destined paths through this same channel.

A soul can come to simply experience months or even weeks of being here. Within those moments, it can experience the oneness of being human through you and serve a purpose that does not require a physical life to live out.

Date:

I am RADIANT.

Date:

I am FULFILLED.

Date:

"Life is always creating for you to experience itself in many ways and those ways are infinite to our souls existence."

I am GENEROUS.

Date:

I am REJUVENATION.

Date:

I am HOPE.

Date:

*I*ntertwined

The days come to an end
And somewhere in my waking dreams I find you alive and
Breathing in my heart

You consume the fragile parts of me
Fear of becoming broken is no longer my concern now
As this, what we have, is worth the risk

Love captures all of my senses to let you take over me
And when the sun dies in the midnight skies
The stars guided you right to me
For forever is all I have with you

My eyes see no life without you existing in it
And my destiny grows dim without you by my side

Is this Possible?

Can I trust this anticipation that builds with every thought,
Every glimpse
Can I trust you to fall in this beam of life with me
I can feel the Divine intertwined in our oneness

Taking away everything that I knew I was and creating its own
Identity that leaves me wondering

Is this what Love feels like?

Is this a glimpse of death, of life, of birth as they are all the same
Here and Yet I am different
How does one become so enraptured without effort

But knowing this is the only need I need
I love you, I love you, I love you
Times a thousand and it is not enough

You are too vast for me to truly capture what you are to me
My thoughts do not convey
But in the stillness of my waking dreams
Every fiber of my existence knows you are there

I am ALIVE.

Date:

I am ELATION.

Date:

"Love transcends time and space."

I am WHOLE.

Date:

I am HARMONIOUS.

Date:

I am EXCEPTIONAL.

Date:

" You are in this physical world and yet also beyond it."

When we have such a spiritual experience that impacts the deepest parts of our souls. That opens us to realms that many of us may not have known existed. We may find ourselves caught in-between the space of eternity and time.

Once you are made aware, it cannot be undone.

With that awareness comes the understanding that there is more happening beyond this physical life than what we can expect from it. This knowing pushes us to reach far into that connection within ourselves and to unlock the possibilities of our own souls journey of being here.

What we See is not the only reality to discover.

Date:

I am FORGIVENESS.

Date:

I am INTUITIVE.

Date:

"See beyond the surface and recognize the infinite connection within."

I am TRUST.

Date:

I am STRENGTH.

Date:

I am VIBRANT.

Date:

" Only in our expectations do we limit the possibilities of what Life can create from us."

Often we are blinded by our expectations of how the situation should or should not be and only in our expectations of life do we find ourselves disappointed.

We suffer from the hope and the expectations of our own limitations of life.

The possibilities of what can be created beyond our hopes and dreams lie in the acceptance that whatever is, is exactly what was destined to be and what is created from this moment is fulfilling the greater purpose of your life. Be open to the limitless nature of life and its ability to create beyond what we think is best for our lives.

Date:

I am CAREFREE.

Date:

I am FORTUNATE.

Date:

"The life that was created is not limited to what it can be. Allow it to give life in all areas of your being."

I am ETERNAL.

Date:

I am APPRECIATIVE.

Date:

I am RESTORED.

Date:

"Be gentle with yourself and Nurture your soul, mind and body through Love."

Though these experiences are common in nature, they are taboo in our culture to speak openly about them. It can become a silent, invisible wound that many women feel ashamed of and never truly heal from.

Give yourself permission to process this experience in its totality and to thoroughly heal. Create the space and environment for self care and support.

Be open to allowing the love that you carried to nurture your being into healing.

Date:

I am KIND.

Date:

I am WORTHY.

Date:

"Breathe. Deeply take in the renewal of your soul and the rejuvenation for your body."

I am CREATION.

Date:

I am ABUNDANCE.

Date:

I am PURE.

Date:

"In the silent moments Listen to your Spirits truth."

The transformation of this experience will unravel the cords of your existence. It brings a change that we have to take the time to discover what that change is from the inside, out.

Seek the truth of the experience. In doing so, you will gain a deeper understanding that offers clarity and peace to the mind.

It is only to our advantage to listen and be guided through every step of the way in moving forward.

Your spirit knows what your mind has yet to understand.

Date:

I am FREEDOM.

Date:

I am EFFERVESCENT.

Date:

"Your Spirit holds the truth that eradicates all the misunderstandings of Life."

I am OPTIMISTIC.

Date:

I am LOVABLE.

Date:

I am AMAZING.

Date:

I love you

I heard you,
I promise I did.

You did not leave without recognition
I saw you falling from the sky
Making belief what I saw only as a fantasy
But I did hear you as though your breath whispered in my ear

That is how close I held you
Felt you even while I slept
Like winds blowing through my hair and the softness of the
Springs touch
It made my heart flutter to imagine your dreams, to see life from
The eyes of your eternity
You flow through my body and your DNA is written on my
Journey

I heard you,
I promise I did.

Never imagining you to be so close to me
But I felt your words embracing my soul
Kissing me gently
You imprinted to be remembered and your life goes without
Forgetting
It will be forever and I will always hear the spoken silence
Those words that illuminate my soul
That traveled miles of lifetimes and finding rest within my body
As I fall asleep as the sun rises

I heard you,
I promise I did.

I love you, too.

Date:

I am COURAGEOUS.

Date:

I am ENERGETIC.

Date:

"Love holds an Eternal life that you will forever be connected to."

I am BEAUTIFUL.

Date:

I am LIMITLESS.

Date:

I am JOY.

Date:

"Be mindful of the narrative you speak to yourself."

How you perceive and how you believe an experience to be is how you will emotionally and physically respond and react to it even as we remember it over time.

The narrative that you find yourself playing over and over in your mind through your hurt and pain can become a habitual feeling that though your life will physically move on, you may find that hurt replaying itself years later, with no purpose in your current state for it to exist.

Allow what you have experienced to evolve through the hurt into a narrative that holds the acceptance, understanding and the truth that it brings as it continues to create the fullness of life within you.

Date:

I am CENTERED.

Date:

I am EXPANSIVE.

Date:

*"Embrace all that was given and
Let go of all that was not."*

I am GIVING.

Date:

I am IMAGINATIVE.

Date:

I am MARVELOUS.

Date:

"A loss is only perceived through the eyes of one that cannot see the abundance of ALL that is life within them."

You are the true nature of all of life that exist. The oneness that connects us all together. One cannot lose what they themselves are created from.

It rains through the trees in the forest

It illuminates throughout the skies in the dark

It blossoms in the fields of a thousand lands

It is the breath of every life that has lived

You are a part of it all. The abundance of life that expands beyond all lives that can be lived.

Date:

I am PERFECT.

Date:

I am HEALED.

Date:

"Be the creator of life that you were created to be."

I am VALUBLE.

Date:

I am GRATEFUL.

Date:

I am NATURAL.

Date:

> *"The truth of Everything is unveiled through the hindsights of time."*

In every moment we are given, time is in constant motion to unveil much of the purpose of why things happen. It is rarely in the present moment, as the moment itself is always part of a greater picture that is being created.

Through Hindsight, we are able to see exactly why things had to happen the way they play out. It serves us well to respond to the happenings of our lives simply as a chapter to the overall story that has yet to be told. To see the story all the way through before we hold truth to what seems to be misunderstood in the moment.

In the end, Life makes no mistakes in how it writes our lives through the eternal purpose of time.

Date:

I am CALM.

Date:

I am LUMINOUS.

Date:

"Trust and know that all you are destined for will come to you in perfect time."

I am BLISS.

Date:

I am PHENOMENAL.

Date:

I am MIRACULOUS.

Date:

www.ingramcontent.com/pod-product-compliance
Lightning Source LLC
Chambersburg PA
CBHW031117080526
44587CB00011B/1004